THE VALUE OF FACING A CHALLENGE
The Story of Terry Fox

MARATHON OF HOPE

VALUE COMMUNICATIONS, INC.
PUBLISHERS
LA JOLLA, CALIFORNIA

THE VALUE OF FACING A CHALLENGE

ILLUSTRATED BY Pileggi

The Story of
Terry Fox

BY ANN DONEGAN JOHNSON

The Value of Facing a Challenge is part of the ValueTales series.

First Edition
Manufactured in the United States of America.
For information write to: ValueTales,
9601 Arrow Drive, San Diego, CA 92123

All dialogue in the text is fictitious.

Library of Congress Cataloging in Publication Data

Johnson, Ann Donegan.
    The value of facing a challenge.

    (ValueTales)
    SUMMARY: A biography of a young cancer patient with
an artificial leg who determined to run 5300 miles
across Canada in his own Marathon of Hope in order to
raise money for cancer research.
    1. Osteosarcoma—Patients—Canada—Biography—
Juvenile literature.   2. Fox, Terry, 1958–1981—Juvenile
literature. [1. Fox, Terry, 1958–1981.   2. Osteosarcoma
—Patients.   3. Cancer—Patients.   4. Courage]
I. Pileggi, Steve, ill.   II. Title.   III. Series.
RC280.B6J63   1983   362.1'9699471'00924 [B] [92]   83-8542

ISBN 0-7172-8134-5

3 4 5 6 7 8 9 84 83

This tale is about Terry Fox,
who faced a great challenge with
courage and determination. The story
that follows is based on events
in his life. More historical facts
about Terry Fox can be found on page 63.

6

Once upon a time...

not very long ago, a boy named Terry Fox was growing up in Port Coquitlam, on Canada's west coast.

In most ways Terry was an ordinary boy. "An average guy," that's how he thought of himself. And like a lot of people, he expected to live an ordinary, average life.

As we shall see, however, that was not to be.

The Foxes were a close, loving family. But all of them—Terry himself, his parents, Rolly and Betty, his brothers, Fred and Darrell, and his sister, Judith—were strong-minded people.

So there was always a lot of debate and discussion as well as a lot of fun and laughter in the Fox household. And Terry, you can be sure, won more than his share of the arguments.

For Terry Fox was average in every way but one.

Terry loved a challenge. Once he started something, he simply would not give up until he had seen it through.

Even as a very small child he had been like that: stacking his blocks over and over again until they stayed the way he wanted.

Later, he invented games and continued playing, even after he would have preferred to quit. Terry always liked to finish what he started.

"Terry, for the last time, will you please come to supper!" his mother would call.

"O.K., Mom," was the usual answer. "I am coming."

Terry set himself many challenges as he was growing up. Basketball was one of them. Terry was small for his age, but he was determined to make the school team.

One day Terry and his friend, Doug Alward, were having a chat after school. Terry suddenly jumped up.

"Come on, Doug," he said. "Enough of this sitting around. Let's go practice some basketball shots before dinner."

"Give me a break!" groaned Doug. "You must be the only guy in eighth grade who thinks basketball twenty-four hours a day." But, as usual, he went.

"By the way," Doug asked as they played, "what did the coach say when you went for the tryouts today?"

"Ah, nothing much," mumbled Terry.

"You seemed pretty upset after school. He must have said something," insisted Doug.

Terry sighed. "Coach said I am too short for basketball. He thinks I'd be better off wrestling."

What the coach didn't know was that telling Terry he couldn't do something was just the kind of challenge that would make him go out and find the way to do it.

Terry worked harder than ever at his basketball. He practiced with Doug, and he even took up cross-country running.

"I hate running," he confided to Doug. "But the coach said it would toughen me up."

To the coach's surprise, Terry improved enough to make the team. He was the last player chosen, and he didn't play much in games at first, but he kept on improving.

Soon Terry was graduating from high school. His father was very proud of him.

"My Terry is certainly something else," he told his friends at the rail yard where he worked. "He got almost straight A's. Yes, sir. It was a real challenge for him, too. And making it on the high school basketball team was even more of a challenge."

Terry's father enjoyed boasting to his friends at the rail yard. "Not only did he make the basketball team," he added, beaming, "but he and his friend Doug shared the Athlete of the Year Award."

13

Rolly Fox had every right to be proud of his son. Terry applied to and was accepted by Simon Fraser University.

"What is this kinesiology you are studying?" his friends would ask him.

"It's the study of body movement," replied Terry.

Terry was as keen as ever on basketball, and once again he made the team through sheer hard work.

But before he finished his first year at the university, something very sad happened.

A pain in his right knee had been bothering Terry for weeks. He had ignored it, determined to finish the basketball season. Now, suddenly, it was so bad he couldn't stand up.

Terry's parents took him to the hospital. Tests showed that Terry had cancer. He was going to lose his leg. When the doctor told him, he cried.

"But I can't lose my leg," he protested. "I am an athlete!"

"I understand how you feel," replied the doctor.

"Nobody could understand how I feel," Terry said quietly.

Of course, Terry was right. Nobody really could, but they certainly tried. His family, his coaches, Doug and his other friends all gave Terry wonderful support. "Knowing that all those people cared really helped me," Terry said later.

16

This was surely the greatest challenge Terry had ever faced in his life.

And Terry did face the challenge, with spirit and determination as always. Barely six weeks later, with an artificial leg and a cane in his hand, Terry visited his dad at work. Rolly's friends were delighted to see Terry looking so well and were astounded by his courage.

"You have quite a son there, Rolly," they said. Rolly didn't have to be told that. He knew it.

"Come on, Dad, let's go play that game of pitch and putt you promised," called Terry.

That same night, Terry thought about what had happened as he sat on the steps outside his parents' home.

"They're all really supportive," he thought, "but it's funny. I am the one who has to cheer everybody up. Even Terry Fleming, my basketball coach, was really down when he came to visit me in the hospital. They don't understand how I feel inside. This is a new challenge and a big one at that. But I can do it!"

Then Terry pulled out a folded magazine article from his pocket. He opened the rumpled paper carefully. The article was from *Runner's World* and the coach had given it to him in the hospital. It was about Dick Traum, who also had an artificial leg and who ran in the New York Marathon. "Well, if he can do it," thought Terry, "I can too! In fact, I am going to do more than run in the New York Marathon."

"I have a dream, a challenge for myself. I am going to run across the whole of Canada, from sea to sea. It will be my Marathon of Hope, and all the money I can raise will go to cancer research."

Do you think Terry could really do it?

For the next sixteen months Terry was in and out of the hospital undergoing special treatment. His experiences at the hospital made him feel an even greater determination to fight cancer. Seeing the courage with which others faced the disease made him want to do something to help them.

It was during this time that Terry met a very special friend. Her name was Rika. She was twenty years old, just like Terry, and as lively as Terry could be shy. Rika helped coach wheelchair volleyball players and had met Terry when he was playing wheelchair basketball.

Terry told Rika of his dream of running across Canada. "I think it's a wonderful idea!" said Rika. "But you are going to need some sponsors." Terry agreed with her.

"Why don't you write to some large companies and explain what you are trying to do," suggested Rika.

"Great idea!" said Terry. He got some notepaper out and started writing letters. He asked the companies to sponsor the Marathon of Hope in whatever way they could.

Terry began to prepare for his marathon. He started by running short distances, but every day he ran a little longer. In seven days Terry was running a mile.

One day, as Terry sat and rested after running, he suddenly thought he heard two little voices.

"Hi there, Terry!" they seemed to say. "Our names are Speedy and Spunky."

Startled, Terry looked down to where the voices seemed to come from. He felt he was imagining things, for there on his running shoes were two smiling little faces looking up at him.

"Don't be startled, Terry," they laughed. "We just want to be your friends."

Terry thought for a moment and said, "Well, faced with this challenge, I am certainly going to need my shoes to be my friends. You will have to carry me a long way."

The two little faces smiled up at Terry. "Don't worry, we won't let you down. You will have a lot more training to do, but you are getting healthy and strong and running hard. You can do it, Terry!"

"Well, I am certainly going to depend on you, my friends," laughed Terry.

23

To test himself, Terry entered the Prince George Marathon. He intended to run only half the distance, but Doug had different plans for Terry.

"Come on, Terry. You can finish," needled Doug, knowing Terry always liked a challenge. Doug nagged a very tired but excited Terry across the finish line.

"You did it! You did it!" cried Speedy and Spunky as Terry smiled happily.

One day, when Rika was out running with Terry, they met a Canadian National Railways switchman who worked with Terry's dad.

"Hi there, Terry," the switchman beamed. "How are you doing?"

"Great," grinned Terry, "thanks to the wheelchair you guys bought me. It has given me terrific mileage."

"Yes, we hear you've been racing your friend Doug out on the track and playing wheelchair basketball. What's next?"

Terry laughed.

Rika piped in proudly, "Terry's on the Vancouver Cablecars Wheelchair Basketball Team. They came in first in the finals."

"With Terry on the team, of course they did," muttered Speedy and Spunky.

"I ran one hundred and one days in a row," admitted Terry with pride. "I might have done even more, but I promised Mom I would take Christmas Day off. It's all part of my training," he added, and then explained his plan to run across Canada to raise money for cancer research. The railway man couldn't believe his ears.

"Why Terry, that's crazy!" he burst out.

Terry sighed. "That's what Mom thought at first."

"And what did your dad have to say?"

"The whole family is with me now," answered Terry happily. "In fact, they have organized garage sales and a dance to raise money for living expenses along the way. They've been terrific."

When the railway man still looked doubtful, Rika spoke up. "I think it's a wonderful idea," she said firmly. "I'll be praying for him."

Terry grinned. "And Doug is going with me. He wasn't a bit surprised when I told him. He just asked when we were leaving."

The day came quickly. After running 3,000 miles in training, Terry boarded a plane for Newfoundland on Canada's east coast. He was ready to take on the challenge of a 5,300-mile run across Canada.

The day Terry started his run, his family and friends watched him on television on the morning news.

There were Terry and Doug in St. John's, Newfoundland. Doug was driving a van donated by the Ford Motor Company that used gas donated by Imperial Oil. The letters had worked! Several other large companies also helped Terry in whatever way they could. Even large companies understand a challenge. A company has to start from scratch, too. Without the help of others, that can be hard. Speedy and Spunky understood that, too.

It was April 12, 1980, and a cold rainy morning. Terry told reporters his challenge was to raise $1,000,000 for cancer research. He hoped to run thirty to forty miles a day and be back home in Port Coquitlam in six months.

One reporter said, "You sound pretty confident."

"If it's only up to me and my mind," Terry answered, "I've got a lot of positive attitude. I think I can do it."

"We don't think you can do it, Terry, we *know* you can," whispered Speedy and Spunky. "We'll be with you all the way!"

Terry looked down at his little friends and smiled.

When Terry began his run, Speedy and Spunky were discussing quietly how they could make it easier for Terry. Spunky was on Terry's artificial leg, and Speedy was on his good leg. "Okay, Terry, how about starting with a double hop on me," suggested Speedy. "And then a long step on me," added Spunky.

"That should work pretty well," said Terry. "Let's give it a try."

Just seeing Terry run, his face filled with determination, warmed the hearts of Canadians.

People began inviting him into their homes for meals. In the first towns he ran through, donations poured in. In one town of 10,000 people, the donations came to a fantastic $10,000.

One dollar per person now became the dream Terry had for his Marathon of Hope.

Things weren't all rosy, of course. Over the next few weeks Terry had many disappointments. He would make it all the way from one town to the next, and often no one was waiting. And that meant no money for cancer research.

Sometimes Terry got really discouraged. But Speedy and Spunky always found a way to cheer him up. "Come on, Terry, there are lots of other towns!" they cried.

Running was hard on Terry. One time he got dizzy and light-headed because the strain on his heart was so great. That really scared him. But the reaction was typical of Terry. He rested a few minutes in the van, then went out and did fifteen push-ups in the road and started running again.

"Great!" encouraged Speedy and Spunky. "Just remember, a double hop and a long step."

Terry's Marathon of Hope collected $40,000 in Newfoundland. Children donated their allowances, and one group wrote a special song to welcome him to their school.

Terry told them, "I bet some of you feel sorry for me. Well, don't. Having an artificial leg has its advantages. I've broken my right knee several times, and it didn't hurt a bit."

The children laughed. They really liked Terry.

Terry liked young people a lot, too. Again and again during Terry's run, young people joined in and ran with him. Terry sometimes turned on the speed and ran as fast as he could to show them just what he could do. They ended up tired and puffing.

One newspaper, the Halifax *Mail Star*, wrote an article on Terry on May 21.

The paper quoted Terry as saying, "People seem to forget what I am doing this for. They think I am running across Canada on some kind of ego trip. It is a personal challenge, but I am trying to raise as much money as I can for cancer research. I need their support."

Terry made steady progress running on Prince Edward Island and then across New Brunswick. The donations kept coming and Terry pounded out the miles no matter how tired he got.

Just the running would have been hard enough on Terry. But he also had to attend press conferences and fund-raising dinners after the day's run was over. Fortunately, Doug and Terry's little friends, Speedy and Spunky, were always there to support him.

"I know you are tired, but these people are donating a lot of money to your cause. It gives them a thrill to see you in person. You owe them that," Speedy reminded Terry.

Terry didn't really need reminding. He understood his responsibilities very well. He went, and most of the time he enjoyed himself.

37

In June, Terry got a wonderful surprise. His younger brother, Darrell, joined him on his Marathon of Hope. Terry was delighted: Darrell was the joker in the family.

"I'll bet you can't do this," chanted Darrell, as he leaped into the air and clicked his heels.

"I don't think I would try that if I were you," warned Spunky.

Terry laughed. "I leave that sort of thing to Darrell."

Having Darrell along really gave Terry's spirits a lift, especially on tough days.

And there were still tough days. Days when they collected almost no money. Days when Terry ran through pouring rain or hailstones the size of golfballs. Days when he nearly got hit by cars.

But there were good days, too.

In Montreal, four wheelchair athletes and a football star, Don Sweet, accompanied Terry through the streets to a reception at City Hall.

The president of an international chain of hotels put the boys up in the luxury suite, and it was like nothing they had experienced before.

"Look at these, will you," marveled Darrell, when their T-shirts came back from the laundry. "Each one is wrapped in paper just as if it were brand new."

39

But it was in the province of Ontario that the Marathon of Hope really got up steam. Hawkesbury, the first town inside the Ontario border, welcomed Terry with cheers, balloons, and a brass band. He got a police escort with lights flashing.

Two young bicyclists, Jim Brown and Garth Walker, met Terry in Ottawa, the capital of Canada. They rode three hundred miles from Toronto in twenty-three hours to bring him more than $50,000 in cash and pledges that they had raised for the Marathon of Hope.

The next day Terry made the official kickoff at a Canadian Football League exhibition game. The crowd of 16,000 gave him a standing ovation.

In Ottawa, Terry also met the Governor General of Canada, Edward Schreyer.

You might think Terry dressed up for the occasion. Well, Terry wore his same old gray flannel shorts and his Marathon of Hope T-shirt. He wanted people to remember what he was running for—cancer research.

He wore these clothes when he met Prime Minister Pierre Elliott Trudeau, too.

In Ontario, Terry's spirits really soared. School children donated the money they raised by saving pennies and nickels from their allowances. Teachers matched the amounts their students gave. Even at dawn and in the rain, people lined the highways waiting for him to pass.

Bus drivers stopped their buses when they saw him. They collected money from their passengers to hand to Doug or Darrell. Terry would wave his thanks as he ran by.

Radio stations and the Canadian TV networks were now covering Terry almost all the time. An American network also told Terry's story. They sent a crew to film him for the program "Real People." The show's hostess, Sarah Purcell, ran with Terry as she interviewed him.

The new challenge for Terry was the challenge of being a celebrity. He was exhausted, but the public wanted to see him. He was nearly mobbed in shopping malls. Everybody wanted to touch him, shake his hand, get his autograph.

"I am an ordinary guy out to challenge cancer. It is the Marathon of Hope you should be thinking about, not me," Terry would remind them.

A wonderful surprise was waiting for Terry just outside the city of Toronto.

Terry was tired and concentrating hard on his running.

Suddenly Speedy and Spunky cried, "Hey Terry, look ahead!"

Terry looked, and there were all his family standing at the side of the road. One of the city's newspapers had flown them in for a reunion with him.

For the next few minutes, everybody was hugging and crying and laughing and asking questions all at once. Then, with his challenge foremost in his mind, Terry set off again, running with his spirits high, his fatigue lifted as if by magic.

The next day brought another surprise. Bill Vigars, who was organizing the run through Ontario, had asked Terry if there was anything special he wanted done in Toronto.

"It would be nice to meet Darryl Sittler and Bobby Orr, my hockey heroes," Terry replied. Mischievously, Bill now told Terry that it looked as if Sittler wouldn't be able to make it.

Imagine Terry's delight then when Sittler turned up at the hotel after breakfast. Wearing red shorts and a Terry Fox T-shirt, he poked his head into Terry's room and casually asked, "Anybody want to go for a run?"

Terry took Toronto by storm as he ran downtown through ninety-degree heat in the lunch hour traffic. People lined the streets, sometimes eight or ten deep, applauding wildly. A wedding party on its way into church turned back and everybody, including the bride, groom, and minister, joined the cheering and the giving. One man got so carried away he gave all the money he was carrying and then had to ask for enough back to pay his bus fare.

So much money was donated that the Cancer Society volunteers couldn't handle it all. More volunteers had to be recruited from the crowds. With large garbage bags, the volunteers dashed back and forth between the crowd on the sidewalk and the cars that stopped anywhere and everywhere so that the drivers could contribute.

The run ended in front of Toronto City Hall, where thousands had gathered to hear Terry speak.

Terry stood on the platform with several celebrities. Darryl Sittler presented him with his National Hockey League All-Star Team sweater. "I've been around athletes a long time," Sittler said, "and I've never seen any with his courage and stamina."

46

The crowds and the fund raising continued as Terry ran through the heavily populated centers of southern Ontario.

Each day's run became a parade of kids, adults, police escorts, film crews, honking cars, and dozens of volunteers dodging around collecting donations. Back in Toronto for a luncheon, Terry met his other hero, Bobby Orr. A large company had given Bobby $25,000 to present to Terry.

The crowds were wonderful, but tiring. The heat was stifling.

As Terry ran, his two little friends kept up their encouraging chatter. "You know, Terry, your example is inspiring people to join together in a common purpose," they pointed out. "It is making people want to try to do something to make the world better."

The knowledge affected Terry deeply. To go on moving people in this way became a new goal and a new challenge.

Terry moved some people to new heights. The inmates of a penitentiary, for example, raised $900 by washing cars for the Marathon of Hope.

Some of the things people did to raise money for Terry could be quite funny. A man from Hamilton raised $912 by sitting for fifty-one hours in a vat of banana-lemon custard. Another man crawled eleven and a half miles on his hands and knees and raised $5,000.

The pressure on Terry eased up when he left southern Ontario. The days were cooler. There were still crowds and dinners and lunches to be faced, but the towns were smaller and farther apart.

Terry arrived in the town of Gravenhurst, Ontario, in time for his twenty-second birthday, and what a birthday surprise Gravenhurst had for him! In a town of 8,000, the citizens donated $14,000. That was almost double Terry's dream of one dollar from each Canadian.

Terry got birthday telegrams from everywhere. One from his home province of British Columbia had one thousand signatures.

About this time, some reporters began writing about how hard the running was on Terry. "Come on, Terry, surely you've done enough," some people were saying. "It's time to quit."

Terry knew they meant well, but he was not about to give up. The harder it was, the greater the challenge. Speedy and Spunky understood how he felt.

"Hey, Speedy, I'm doing just great!" shouted Spunky. "How are you doing?"

"If Terry can hang in, I certainly can. After all, that is what we are here for," replied Speedy.

53

Terry was determined to prove that those who said he should quit were wrong. People had been warning him ever since Toronto that a particular hill in northern Ontario would be tough.

The van waited for Terry halfway up the hill, where he normally would have stopped for a short rest.

Imagine everyone's surprise when Terry just ran right by them! He ran all the way to the top without a break.

"Is that it?" he grinned victoriously at the top.

"A piece of cake, Terry, a piece of cake," laughed Speedy and Spunky.

In and out of the towns, people still lined the streets and highways to see and greet Terry.

"Go, Terry, go!" they shouted. "You can do it, Terry!"

But towns were now few and far between. One day there was nobody to be seen until a pick-up truck loaded with Indians from a nearby community passed by. The Indians waved and cheered.

A few minutes later the same truck reappeared. It came back again and again—each time with a new group of people waving and shouting encouragement. The truck was bringing loads of people to see Terry run and to cheer him on.

55

Then, outside Thunder Bay, Ontario, Terry felt a sharp pain in his chest.

He was just eighteen miles outside the city and a cheering crowd lined the road. Terry didn't want to disappoint them. He ran.

Terry ran eight miles and rested fifteen minutes. The pain in his chest kept up. He got up and ran some more. Speedy and Spunky became very concerned. "We can go all the way with you, Terry, but you'd better find out what this is all about first."

Terry appreciated the encouraging words, but he knew he had run his last mile. He went into the van and told Doug to get him to the hospital.

What was wrong? Was it Terry's leg? Was it his heart?

No, it was Terry's old enemy striking again. This time the cancer was in his lungs.

Within a few hours, Terry's parents were by his side in Thunder Bay. There was a private jet ready to take him home. At a press conference before he left Thunder Bay, Terry told reporters, "I'll fight. I promise I won't give up. I just hope the fund raising will continue."

And continue it did!

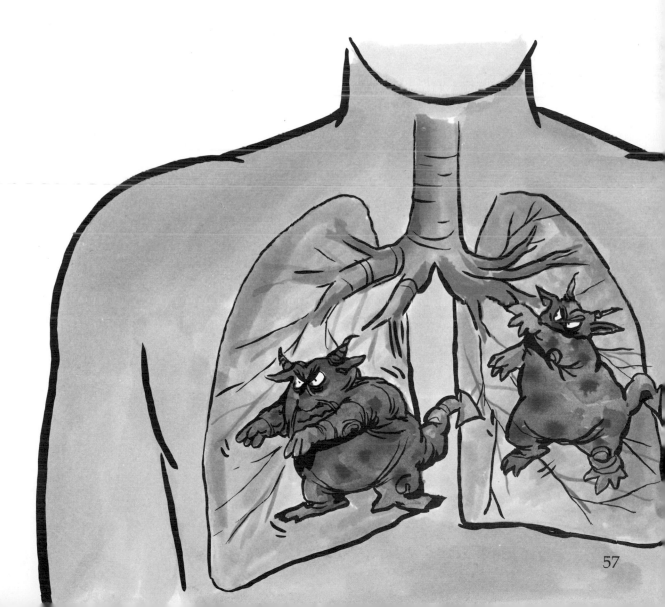

In only five days, a nationwide telecast was organized, a tribute to Terry Fox.

Terry watched the telecast and couldn't believe his eyes. Stars like John Denver, Anne Murray, Elton John, Glen Campbell, Gordon Lightfoot, and Nana Mouskouri were singing for him. Karen Kain, Canada's prima ballerina, danced for him.

By the end of the night, the people of Canada had pledged or donated $10.5 million to Terry's Marathon of Hope.

Terry's own marathon might be over, but the Marathon of Hope was thriving.

Over the next months, Terry faced the new challenge, and as he had promised, he fought hard.

Terry studied the Bible a lot during those months. "I guess by believing in God you can't lose," he told reporters.

Do you think people forgot Terry Fox as the months went by?

Absolutely not! Terry became a most honored man. At age twenty-two, he was the youngest Canadian ever to receive Canada's highest civilian award, the Companion of the Order of Canada.

He received many other awards, too, including one from the American Cancer Society. A stamp honoring Terry's achievements was issued. His portrait was enshrined in the Canadian Sports Hall of Fame.

September 13 was designated as Terry Fox Marathon of Hope Day. Every year on that day Canadians would run, jog or walk ten kilometers—six and one-quarter miles—to raise money for cancer research.

Thousands of letters and messages poured in to Terry from people from all over the world. Some were from important people, like Pope John Paul II and the president of the United States, Jimmy Carter. Most were from ordinary people whose hearts were touched by Terry. Some were simply addressed to Terry Fox, General Delivery, Canada.

Terry Fox died on Sunday, June 28, 1981. It's hard not to be sad about this. But the important thing to remember is what Terry did with his life.

Terry never let himself sit around and be sad. Instead, he went out and met the challenge.

Terry didn't reach his goal of running across Canada. But he did reach the goal that was most important to him. He made millions of people all over the world aware of the need for cancer research. He raised more money than he had ever hoped he would.

"Dreams are made if people try," Terry said. Well, he certainly proved it. He proved that the individual, the ordinary "little guy," can make a difference.

If you accept the challenge to give your best no matter what the odds against you, then you too can make a difference—just like our good friend, Terry Fox.

The End

Terry Fox was born in 1958 in Winnipeg, Manitoba, Canada. When he was ten years old the family moved to Port Coquitlam, British Columbia. There, in this suburb of Vancouver, Terry grew up with his brothers, Fred and Darrell, and his sister, Judith.

According to Terry's mother, he was "average in everything but determination." His great love was basketball. Although he was not very talented and his coaches considered him too short for the game, he earned himself a place on his school basketball teams by working hard and never giving up.

After graduating from high school, Terry enrolled at Simon Fraser University to major in kinesiology, the study of human movement. He immediately tried out for the junior basketball team and once again made the team by sheer drive.

In December 1976, during his first year at the university, Terry noticed a pain in his right knee. He thought it was the result of playing so much basketball and, for fear of having to stop playing, decided to tell no one about it until after the season was over.

In March Terry's problem was diagnosed as osteosarcoma, a relatively rare bone cancer. It was decided that he would have to be operated on and three days later, his right leg was amputated above the knee.

After the initial shock of hearing the diagnosis, Terry amazed his family and friends by his positive attitude. When his coach, Terry Fleming, showed him an article about a one-legged man, Dick Traum, who had run the New York Marathon, Terry decided there and then that he too could do it. In fact he decided to do even more, to run all the way across Canada, over 5,000 miles.

His idea of a cross-Canada run did not fade over the following months as Terry underwent treatments and learned first to walk, then to run, with an artificial leg. Rather, the idea grew and acquired a new purpose. Terry was deeply moved by the suffering and the courage of the other cancer patients he saw at the hospital. Terry decided that his run would be more than a personal marathon to prove that his physical handicap had not disabled him. It would be a

TERRY FOX
1958–1981

Marathon of Hope through which he would raise as much money as he could for cancer research.

Over the next two and one-half years Terry resumed his university studies and spent almost all his spare time building up strength and stamina and preparing for his run.

Finally, in the spring of 1980, he was ready. His parents, apprehensive at first, had come around and had even helped raise money for living expenses along the way. Several large companies had agreed to help by supplying a van and gas and running shoes.

Terry's Marathon of Hope began in St. John's, Newfoundland, on April 12, 1980. By the time it ended four and one-half months and 3,339 miles later, Terry had raised over $2 million for cancer research. After the run ended, the figure climbed to nearly $25 million, or more than the one dollar per Canadian that was his goal.

But Terry Fox gave the world much more than can be counted in dollars and cents. By his selfless response to his own misfortune and his conviction that the ordinary "little guy" can make a difference, by his commitment to his purpose and his faith in the human spirit, he taught us something new about facing the challenge of living life to the full. He became a symbol of hope and courage to millions in Canada and throughout the world.

The ValueTale Series